# MEDICAL SCHOOL INTERVIEW HANDBOOK

## E F WILLIAMS & A TAYLOR

# TABLE OF CONTENTS

## 01 Work Experience and Reflection 06

How to get work experience 07
Work experience diary 09
Reflection examples▲ 10
Reflection template 13
Reflection practice questions* 14
Topics to reflect on * 15
Qualities of a doctor 16

## 02 Core Interview Knowledge 17

NHS core principles 18
The 6 Cs 19
Abbreviations and definitions 20
Medical research terminology* 22
Medical research practice questions* 24
Thinking outside the box *▲ 25

## 03 Medical School Research 27

Researching medical schools * 28

## 04 Medical Ethics 30

Pillars of ethics 31
Confidentiality *▲ 32

* Practice questions
▲ Example answer

# TABLE OF CONTENTS

04 **Medical Ethics** *(cont)*                32

The patient's role in their care            34
Capacity                                     35
Ethics questions *▲                          36
Ethics template                              39
Value of a human life *                      40

05 **NHS and Health Topics**                 43

Antibiotic resistance *                      44
Type 2 diabetes *                            45
Dementia *                                   46
Measles *                                    47
Stop smoking campaigns *                     48
Sugar tax *                                  49
Organ donation *                             50
7-Day NHS *                                  51
NHS in the winter *                          52
Metabo law *                                 53
Postcode lottery *                           54
Virtual and phone consultations *           55
Ageing population *                          56
What is in the news?                         57
COVID-19 practice questions *                58

* Practice questions
▲ Example answer

# TABLE OF CONTENTS

## 06 Realities of Being a Doctor    59

| | |
|---|---|
| Medical training in the UK | 60 |
| Different medical specialties | 61 |
| Who doctors work with | 63 |
| Easily confused terms | 64 |
| Multidisciplinary teams | 66 |
| Teamwork and leadership | 68 |
| The difficulties of medicine | 70 |
| Dealing with mistakes and feedback | 71 |
| Breaking bad news ▲ | 72 |

## 07 Talking About Yourself    75

| | |
|---|---|
| Your personal statement | 76 |
| Motivation to study medicine | 78 |
| Extracurricular activities and hobbies ▲ | 79 |
| "Why should we give you an offer?" * | 82 |
| "What if you do not get an offer?" * | 84 |
| What to say if you are a graduate | 85 |

## 08 The Interview    86

| | |
|---|---|
| The few days before your interview | 87 |
| Tips for your interview | 88 |
| Using your time wisely | 90 |
| Most common mistakes | 91 |

\* Practice questions
▲ Example answer

# TABLE OF CONTENTS

## 09 Revision and Practice     92

Explain these terms *     93
Recall revision *     94
Medical training pathway quiz *     95
Quiz *     96
Breaking bad news practice *     97
MMI mock 1 *     98
MMI mock 2 *     99

* Practice questions
▲ Example answer

# WORK EXPERIENCE AND REFLECTION

Work experience is a common topic in interviews. The main reason that people perform badly in these types of questions is because they don't know how to properly reflect on their work experience. A good foundation is to have a structure to approach questions on work experience. That way, no matter what the question is on the day, you'll have a system that you can use to answer the questions. Having a structure also allows you to talk about a topic with confidence and without having to over-rehearse it in a way that sounds robotic.

In this chapter, we discuss:
- How to get work experience
- Work experience diary
- Reflection examples
- Reflection template
- Reflection practice questions
- Topics to reflect on
- Qualities of a doctor

# How To Get Work Experience

**See if there is anyone at your college/university to help you with applying for work experience**

Some schools have people to help you apply to work experience and volunteering opportunities. For example, the careers team or someone in charge of medical school applications. Find out early as these services can get busier nearer to the application time.

**Contact as many people as possible**

Many places will not respond to your emails so try to cast a wide net and contact multiple places. If they do not respond to your email, you can try calling and chasing up. Don't be disheartened if you do not get a reply as most places are extremely busy. This is why it is good to contact as many places as possible.

**Research what type of work experience your medical school wants**

Some medical schools have specific criteria for what they consider work experience, e.g. some places do not count virtual work experience, some have a minimum hour of work experience needed, or specific criteria about hands-on caring experience. For other schools, the type of experience is less important and they focus more on reflecting on the skills that you have developed through your experience.

# How To Get Work Experience

**Try and apply to work experience in allied health professional roles**

Work experience shadowing physiotherapists and pharmacists tend to be less competitive and also allow you to talk about why you want to be a doctor over an allied health professional in your interview as you have experienced healthcare roles other than doctors.

**Long work experience is better, but any work experience is better than none**

Try to get long-term work experience over weeks or months. However, if you get a 1 day or 3 day work experience opportunity you can still get a lot out of it as long as you reflect on your experience.

**Work experience where you have a role is better than passive shadowing**

Both are good, but if you volunteer and play a role in the team it can make you appear passionate and help you reflect on being a team member. In fact, some medical schools have a cap on how many hours of doctor shadowing they will accept.

**Try to get community-based work experience**

These can be less competitive than hospital experiences and allow you to play a role rather than just shadow. This will also give you an opportunity to gain communication skills.

# Work Experience Diary

**Which work experience is this?**     **Date/s:**

_____     _____

**Write about something you saw/did that could be improved**

**Write about something you saw/did that was good**

**Write about how you/someone else faced a problem and overcame it**

**How did this placement change your perception of what a doctor does or your motivation to go into medicine?**

# Reflection Examples

## 'Talk about a time where you displayed poor communication.'

### When did you see/display this?

On my work experience on an elderly care ward.

### What happened?

I went to talk to a patient with dementia and found it really difficult. It was particularly difficult knowing how long to wait for before speaking and I kept interrupting them.

### What did you learn?

I ended up staying with this patient for an hour so I could have a conversation with them and practice how to talk to them.

Generally everyday conversations are back and forth with both people talking. I did not have any prior experience of talking to someone with dementia, so I found that I was constantly interrupting this patient, who needed longer pauses to come up with responses.

But as I spent more time with this patient I learnt that giving them longer pauses allowed them to talk without me interrupting. This also allowed them to steer the conversation to whatever they wanted to talk about, which I could tell made the patient a lot more comfortable.

### Why is this relevant to being a doctor?

As a doctor you will see a lot of patients with dementia so it is really important to know how to communicate with them.

I learnt that patients with dementia can have a delayed response and may take longer to process thoughts and language, so it is important to give them this time to speak.

I noticed that giving the patient time to speak allowed them to get their thoughts and feelings across. For example, they were able to tell me that they were thirsty so I could bring them a cup of water. This is important in medicine as it allows patient centred care. The experience showed me that it is important to change how I communicate with people and that is something that would be an extremely important skill as a doctor.

# Reflection Examples

'Talk about a time where you had to work under pressure.'

## When did you see/display this?

I was a team leader for a volunteering project at a local group for adults with autism. We were refurbishing an old room to be used for music therapy. We were reaching our deadline in 2 weeks and due to last minute drop-outs we were behind schedule. Some of these people were meant to do jobs and some were in charge of fundraising.

## What happened?

I spoke to my team about which jobs they could do in addition to their current roles and what additional time they could sacrifice. After this meeting I realised that we could still not reach our goal. I reached out to another volunteer group and asked if they could donate money, objects or volunteers.

## What did you learn?

I learnt about how important it is to ask for help, especially when the results impact people other than me.

It was really interesting being in a leadership role, and the biggest thing I improved on regarding leadership skills is probably my ability to delegate tasks. I could have taken on the extra jobs myself but it would not have been practical and also would not utilise everyone's skills.

## Why is this relevant to being a doctor?

In medicine the patient is the priority. So although it can be difficult to ask for help, it is necessary to accomplish the team's goals, especially in circumstances where not asking for help can bring harm to the patient.

Everyone will have different skills and giving yourself too much work can cause burnout, so being able to delegate is important in medicine for a good MDT.

# Reflection Examples

**'Tell me about a time where you witnessed the realities of medicine in your work experience.'**

## When did you see/display this?

On my NICU work experience where I shadowed a foundation doctor.

## What happened?

The doctor was on her third 14-hour shift and needed to insert a cannula into a preterm baby. Her hands were shaking and she failed three attempts. She then needed to call the registrar to do it instead.

## What did you learn?

One of the realities of medicine that I saw in this experience was that long working hours can take a toll, making it much harder to concentrate and complete tasks.

After speaking to this doctor, I found out that she was incredibly tired and had not eaten in hours. This showed me how overwhelming the role of a doctor can be at times and how important it is to take time to rest and take care of yourself, especially after back-to-back shifts.

## Why is this relevant to being a doctor?

As a doctor, you cannot effectively and safely carry out your duties to your patients if you do not look after yourself first. Long shifts, night shifts and back-to-back shifts are something that all doctors need to be able to manage in a healthy way.

Competence is one of the core values of being a doctor. It is therefore important to make sure that you are able to carry out tasks safely and know when to ask for help when you can't.

# Reflection Template

Put the interview question here:

| When did you see/display this? | What happened? |
|---|---|
| | |

| What did you learn? | Why is this relevant to being a doctor? |
|---|---|
| | |

# Reflection Practice Questions

 Once you have had a practice with the common topics, try and answer these questions timed (6 minutes per station).

---

**Station 1**

**"What do you think are the biggest drawbacks of being a doctor?"**

**"How do you plan on overcoming these?"**

**"What is your greatest weakness?"**

---

**Station 2**

**"What are the components of good communication?"**

**"How would you adapt your communication to a patient with dementia?"**

**"Tell me of a time where communication was a challenge for you?"**

# ✓ Topics To Reflect On

Each of the topics below can be made into practice questions about your work experience or just an experience you had. For each topic make it into a question like 'tell me of a time that you displayed/ witness/ improved on ....'

- [ ] Breaking bad news
- [ ] MDT/teamwork
- [ ] Leadership
- [ ] Patient dignity
- [ ] How to cope with failure/feedback
- [ ] Managing stress/burnout/resilience
- [ ] Building a rapport with patients
- [ ] Coping with death of a patient
- [ ] Active listening
- [ ] Ethical dilemma
- [ ] Working under pressure
- [ ] Empathy
- [ ] Managing time & knowing when to seek help
- [ ] Role of a doctor

# Qualities of a Doctor

Spend a few minutes making a list or mind map on the qualities that would make a good doctor or the ideal medical school applicant, and why that is.

Now think about how many of these qualities relate to you, and think about the following:

- What qualities do you have? What qualities do you not have?
- How will you improve on the qualities that you have? How will you pick up the qualities that you do not have?
- Maybe you have already improved on some, if so how did you improve? Why does this make you more suited to being a doctor?

Reassess yourself in a few weeks time to see if you have improved on any of the qualities, or if you have picked up new ones, and think about why this makes you a better suited candidate to become a doctor. Remember the importance of reflection in driving self-improvement.

---

For example, here we discuss teamwork and how an individual may improve their teamworking abilities.

**Teamwork:**
- Maybe you have played a team sport in the past, or maybe you have participated in a group project of some sort. It does not have to be big or small as long as it relates to the quality such as teamwork.
- If you do not have experience of this, maybe consider joining a team, whether it's a sports team, a debate team or a group presentation. Remember that no activity is bad, and it is all about being able to learn from what you do.
- Reflect on the good aspects of your teamwork experience and the bad aspects.
- Maybe you were able to naturally take lead and delegate tasks to your teammates based on their strengths and weaknesses. However, perhaps you did not appreciate the important of listening, but working on this team made you realise just how important listening is to teamwork.

---

Once you have done this, try to answer mock interview questions about reflecting on weaknesses and discuss the topic that you have been working on.

# CORE INTERVIEW KNOWLEDGE

Interviewers understand that applicants will not have a great amount of medical knowledge. However, applicants would be expected to have a minimum level of scientific knowledge from GCSE and A-Levels or equivalent. This is more of a requirement in some medical schools than others so it is a good idea to look into what the medical school wants to see in the candidate.

It is also useful to be confident with some keywords and terminology related to medicine and the NHS as this will help set you apart from other applicants and help to demonstrate your knowledge of medicine as a career.

In this chapter we will discuss:
- NHS core principles
- Abbreviations and definitions
- Medical research terminology
- Medical research practice questions
- Thinking outside the box

# NHS Core Principles

## Working together for patients

Whatever we do, we do for our patients, and the patients are our priority.

## Respect and dignity

We value all our patients, their families, carers and our staff. We treat them with respect and aim to honour their priorities and needs.

## Commitment to quality of care

We strive to provide the highest quality of care to our patients, and to respect the trust they place in our services.

## Compassion

Compassion is the core of our services, and we ensure to respond with kindness to help every individua going through a difficult time.

## Everyone counts

Our services are for everyone and we use our resources to serve the whole community. We make sure no one is left behind of discriminated against.

## Improving lives

We strive to improve the health and wellbeing of all our service users, as well as their experience of using the NHS.

# The 6 Cs

The 6 Cs are set of values underpinning compassion in practice for all health and social care workers in the NHS.

## Care

This is our main objective through which we help patients and the society and provide consistent care to all our patients.

## Commitment

This is at the heart of what we do and helps us to provide patient care day in and day out.

## Compassion

Helps us to build relationships, empathise and treat everyone with dignity and respect.

## Communication

Core skill in providing good team-based and patient-centred care. Communication is central to teamwork.

## Competence

Central to safe patient care, and enables us to prevent unintentional harm to the patients and staff alike.

## Courage

Enables us to do the right thing, and also helps us to support others through difficult times.

# Abbreviations And Definitions

## Resilience

Ability to cope with difficulties and hardships and remain committed to goals. This is really important in a career like medicine which offers many physical and emotional challenges.

## Dignity

The fundamental right of patients to feel respected and valued as a person, regardless of their ability to communicate this. A simple act of kindness, but it offers an important step in providing good quality care.

## Empathy

The ability to use personal experiences to share the feelings of another individual, acknowledging and understanding what they are going through.

## Holistic care

Patient-centred care that encompasses both medical and non-medical aspects such as physical, social, emotional, psychological and spiritual needs and considerations.

## Informed consent

The patient must be given all reasonable risks, benefits and alternatives to an intervention or treatment and have the capacity to understand these before consenting.

## Gillick competence

An assessment used to determine whether a child under 16 is able to consent to their own medical treatment without parental consent.

# Abbreviations And Definitions

## Confidentiality

Withholding any information about a patient from anyone else wherever appropriate. Though an important ethical and legal consideration, some exceptions apply.

## Capacity

A patient's ability to understand the benefits and risks and any alternatives of a particular medical test or treatment in order to make and communicate a decision.

## Euthanasia

Deliberately ending an individual's life with the intention of relieving suffering. Can be voluntary (when the patient themselves makes this decision) or involuntary (when this decision is made on behalf of the patient by somebody else). e.g. if a doctor administers an agent to end an individual's life. This is illegal in the UK and many other countries.

## Assisted dying

Deliberately assisting somebody to end their own life by providing them the means to do so e.g. if a doctor or relative provides an individual a drug to end their life, knowing that the individual intends to use it for that purpose. This is also illegal in the UK and many other countries. It is legal in some countries e.g. Switzerland.

## Burnout

Being emotionally, mentally and physically exhausted as a result of work-related stress to the point of severely reduced motivation and possible psychological distress, where the individual may consider leaving the role as they no longer feel joy from it.

## MDT

A multidisciplinary team - a group of professionals (normally from more than one discipline) who work together to make decisions to direct patient-centred care.

# Medical Research Terminology

### Clinical trial

The stage of researching new treatment where the experimental treatment (e.g. medicine) is given to participating patients with the disease to see if it works as intended. All medical treatments have to undergo clinical trials in order to be sure that the treatment is both safe and effective at treating the disease.

### Placebo

An alternative to the actual treatment (usually a dummy treatment) which makes participants think they are receiving treatment when they are really being given dummy treatment which does not work.

### Bias

A tendency to support one outcome over another which skews the data in favour of one of the outcomes being tested. This can be a preformed opinion or prejudice that participants may have, or it can be due to differences in accuracies of the equipment being used to test the different groups. There are many different types of biases in research but you do not need to know every single type. The important thing is to understand the concept.

# Medical Research Terminology

**Randomised controlled trial**

A type of clinical trial where the participants are assigned to two or more groups to compare the different treatments. The treatments can be compared with each other or against a placebo. This type of study offers one of the most accurate forms of data on how well a treatment works.

**Single-blinded**

A subtype of randomised controlled trials where the participants do not know which group they belong to, so there is less risk of bias.

**Double-blinded**

A subtype of randomised controlled trials where both the participants and the researchers do not know which groups the participants are in, which minimises the risk of bias.

**Evidence based medicine**

This refers to the practice of modern medicine where decisions about patient care are made using the best quality of evidence to show that the test or treatment works.

# Medical Research Practice Questions

**Practice questions:**

**Why is a double-blinded randomised controlled trial a good way to test if a new drug works?**

**If a new drug is being made, how would you test it before it is used in clinical practice?**
*Hint: Think about both efficacy and safety. A drug should be able to do its job while being safe for the patients.*

**When may a doctor not use evidence-based medicine and what are the implications?**
*Hint: Think about the start of the Covid-19 pandemic*
*Hint: Refer to the section on medical ethics.*

It is a good idea to think of the different concepts as a group as they all relate to each other in some way. For example, medical ethics relates to clinical trials. Thinking in this way will help you to strengthen your answer and demonstrate your knowledge and understanding.

# Thinking Outside The Box

Some medical schools like to ask curveball questions in order to examine your reasoning skills. These questions can appear strange and you may not be expected to know the answer to them. However, what they are assessing is your problem-solving ability. It is important to approach these types of questions methodically so that you can demonstrate your thought process.

Here are some lateral thinking questions for you to practice through. On the next page is an example to give you an idea of how to approach it. Each person has their own technique for approaching these, so have some practice to find what approach works for you for your interview.

**What technology do you think will exist in 50 years?**

**How do you think medicine in the UK will be different in 30 years?**

**How does an astronaut exercise in space?**

# Thinking Outside The Box

**What will be some of the long term health impacts of the climate crisis?**

So for this questions they don't expect you to know much about the climate crisis except basics from science classes. So instead of listing off answers, this question is designed for you to get a small amount of knowledge you know and build on it using different types of knowledge and lateral thinking.

So find a foundation of knowledge, in this case, brainstorm what you know about climate change:
- Extremes of temperature
- Erratic unpredictable weather
- Breaking down of the ozone layer

Now try to build on this with your medical knowledge.

Erratic weather means it will be harder to grow crops, meaning there will be food scarcity, meaning malnutrition.

Hot weather and broken ozone means more sunlight so could increase the risk of skin cancer.

People migrating due to extreme weather like hurricanes could mean overpopulation in migrant camps leading to outbreaks of infectious diseases.

There is no one correct answer to these types of questions. Just make sure that you explain your workings out as you go along, stay on topic and can explain your answer.

# MEDICAL SCHOOL RESEARCH

Knowing what medical schools you like is important when considering which medical schools to apply to and which offers to accept.  It is also important to know for your interview as it is becoming more common for medical schools to ask questions about the medical school, their teaching styles, the location of the medical school and the general population of the area. This is to weed out students who have applied to medical schools without much thought and for the interviewer to find out which students are truly passionate to study at their medical school.

Don't forget to also read about what qualities the medical school is looking for in the interview candidate. Each medical school will likely declare this information on their website so have a look! Once you have done that, read our section on the qualities of a doctor and try the exercise for yourself.

In this chapter we discuss:
- What you need to know about each medical school you are applying for
- Mock questions about medical schools and their location to practice

# Researching Medical Schools

MEDICAL SCHOOL:

Overall score:
☆☆☆☆☆

### What do you like about their teaching style?

e.g. early patient contact, cadaveric dissection, integrated, PBL etc.

### What do you like about the unversity?

e.g. Good student feedback, high national average scores, student support etc.

### What do you like about the location? *

e.g. good student population, near family, city/countryside etc.

### What is the population nearby like?

e.g. elderly population, homelessness, poverty, etc.

### What hospitals work with the university?

### What extracurriculars are there?

e.g. sports clubs, societies, pub quizzes/game nights, music/arts etc.

*Good for you to consider when applying, but be careful bringing up these factors in the interview as answers like 'I can live with my family so I will save money on rent' is not a good reason for the medical school to give you an offer. However, being close to the family for other reasons may be beneficial, so have a think about this.

# Researching Medical Schools

Give a list of the medical schools to which you are applying to a friend and get them to ask you these questions.

**What advantages are there of the teaching methods that this university uses?**

**What about this medical school stood out to you?**

**Do you think cadaveric dissection is important for medical students?**

**Are you aware of the catchment area of the teaching hospitals that this medical school has?**

**What societies at this university would you want to join?**

**If you were a doctor at the local hospital what would be**
**some of the health issues you would see?**

**If you have £1 million to help the health of the local population, what would you spend it on?**

# MEDICAL ETHICS

Medical ethics is important to grasp for you interview as it can be a popular discussion topic. It is one of the topics where it can be very clear to the interviewer who has done their practice and research and who hasn't.

Medical ethics is also important because healthcare professionals come across ethical issues everyday, so having an understanding of this will greatly help you to stand out in your interviews.

There are many common mistakes people make which we will try and help you avoid in this chapter. A very important thing to know is key words and definitions and if you have not grasped this you will struggle if a medical ethics question comes up in your interview.

In this chapter, we discuss:
- Pillars of ethics
- Confidentiality
- The patient's role in their care
- Capacity
- Ethics questions
- Ethics template
- The value of a human life

# Pillars Of Medical Ethics

## Beneficence

Doing what is in the **best interest** of the patient (or the community).
This involves considering whether a particular action or decision would benefit the patient clinically, emotionally or psychologically?

## Non-maleficence

Only take actions that will **not harm** the patient directly or indirectly (or the community).
This involves considering whether a particular action or decision would bring any harm (physical or emotional distress) to the patient?

## Autonomy

Respecting the patient's **right to refuse** treatment or intervention (even if against medical advice) or respecting patient's personal wishes (i.e. request for a female doctor) wherever appropriate.

## Justice

Treating each patient with equity - providing **equal, fair access to healthcare for all** and ensuring that all medical decisions are compatible with the law, the patient's own rights and can be deemed 'fair and balanced'.

## Dignity

While not strictly a principle of medical ethics, dignity is an important concept to know about as it touches open the four pillars above. Dignity means to treat each patient with respect a without prejudice as well as ensuring that each decision taken would be in service of what is best for the patient. This includes  the patient's own choice and involves consideration of the quality of life in context of the medical condition.

# Confidentiality

Confidentiality is the principle of keeping secure and secret information that pertains to a patient or that shared by a patient.

## Benefits of keeping it

- Maintain good doctor-patient relationship.
- Maintain **patients' trust** in medical profession.
- Patient more likely to be honest about clinically relevant information - quicker diagnosis & treatment.
- Patient likely to follow-up/seek further medical attention when required.

## Negatives of breaking it

- Impairs good doctor-patient relationship.
- Patient may **lose trust** in doctor or medical profession.
- Patient may **withhold information** that is vital for diagnosis & treatment.
- Patient may not seek further medical attention when required in the future.

## When may you break confidentiality?

- When patient or other people may be in **harm's way**, e.g. abuse, human trafficking.
- When patient has a notifiable disease e.g. tuberculosis.
- When patient has an infectious disease for which contacts should seek medical help (e.g. notifying sexual partners of STIs).
- Essentially, when a doctor's duty to society supersedes their duty to a patient.

**Practice question:**

**Your patient has recently been diagnosed with epilepsy and asks that you do not share this diagnosis with anyone. What would you do in this situation?**

*Look on the next page to see how to answer this question.*

# Confidentiality

**Your patient has recently been diagnosed with epilepsy and asks that you do not share this diagnosis with anyone. What would you do in this situation?**

This is a good example of a question which requires you to think laterally. A question like this would likely assess your reasoning skills and not your knowledge.

*For this question you need to have very little knowledge of epilepsy:*
- Epilepsy is a common condition which causes seizures, which can lead to individuals losing muscle control and consciousness.

*Next think about how epilepsy affects people (only one example is given here):*
- People with epilepsy are not allowed to drive for a period of time. Even if you did not know this fact, you can think outside the box and infer that a condition like epilepsy can affect the ability to drive, and that there may be laws surrounding this.

*Now think outside the box and consider whether driving with epilepsy may have a knock-on effect:*
- Having a seizure while driving can increase the risk of a collision and therefore endanger the lives of both the patient and the general population.

*Now think about the benefits and risks of maintaining confidentiality here:*
- Benefit: improved doctor-patient relationship and trust.
- Risk: Patient may drive and endanger themselves and members of the public.

So in this case a doctor may have to break confidentiality to report to the DVLA, which is in the best interest of the patient and the public.

# The Patient's Role In Their Care

## Demanding treatment

A patient cannot demand treatment that the clinician does not think is beneficial. A good example of this is demanding antibiotics at the GP for a sore throat when antibiotics are not needed. Patients can instead make a choice on what type of treatment they would like out of the available options.

## Refusing treatment

A patient is allowed to refuse treatment even if the doctor disagrees with their decision as long as they have capacity. For example refusing a blood transfusion.

## Informed Consent

Making sure the risk and benefits are fully explained to the patient for them to weigh out. Give them the opportunity to ask any questions.

**What pillars of medical ethics do the above relate to?**

Read the ethics section later on in the handbook to help you answer this question. Some of the concepts relate to each other so it is good to think of the different concepts as a group. This will help you strengthen your answer and demonstrate your understanding.

# Capacity

## Capacity

Having capacity means the patient is able to:

- Remember what you have told them long enough to make a decision.
- Understand the risks and benefits.
- Weigh up the pros and cons.
- Communicate their decision.

## Lack of capacity

Here are some examples of scenarios where someone may have a lack of capacity.

- Being drunk
- Being in a coma/unconscious
- Being confused e.g. dementia
- Mental health conditions e.g. schizophrenia, suicidal
- Learning disability
- Brain damage e.g. after a stroke or head injury
- Children (sometimes)

**Why do you think these can cause a lack of capacity?**

## Who has capacity?

We assume everyone over 16 has capacity unless they have a disease of the mind or brain that makes us question if they lack capacity. We then need to assess capacity. Remember that capacity is specific for one decision. For example, someone without capacity may not be able refuse treatment but they can still choose their dinner.

# Ethics Questions

**Put the interview question here:**
What are the ethics of a 14 year old girl asking her GP for for the oral contraceptive pill?

## Non-maleficence

If the doctor did **not** prescribe the medication and the 14 year old girl got pregnant, it can be argued that the pregnancy would put the girl in more harm than prescribing the pill.

## Beneficence

By prescribing the medication, the doctor is acting in the patient's **best interest**, which is to avoid getting pregnant.

## Justice

As always, it is important to treat each patient without prejudice.

## Autonomy / Consent

If you can assess that the child has Gillick competence, then the doctor is able to respect the patient's autonomy and provide them with contraceptive advice.

## Dignity

You should not be judgemental or impose your own personal views on the patient as this can affect the doctor-patient relationship and undermine the patient's trust in the medical profession.

Any other points

**Overall, my opinion is** If the patient was assessed to be Gillick-competent, I would be happy prescribing them the pill after having a detailed discussion with them about the pros and cons of different contraceptives and the consequences of unprotected sex.

# Ethics Questions

When answering ethical questions it is important to:

- Always talk about both sides of an argument. This is especially important for emotive questions where there may be an answer that seems 'obviously correct' to you.
- Try to make points about the individual, society and the NHS where possible to be as holistic as you can.
- Use the key words surrounding principles of ethics. The marker will notice when you bring them up.
- Talk through your thought process outload, as most of the points will come from justification rather than your answer itself.
- Do not be judgemental.
- Use famous cases, laws or public health campaigns where relevant. If there is an ethical scenario regarding the UK that has already occurred in another country, mention that.
- Give your opinion at the end. You can appreciate that a scenario is complicated but still give an answer and don't be on the fence.

# Ethics Questions

☐ Do you think we should introduce a fat tax?

☐ Do you think we should legalise euthanasia?

☐ Do you think we should make vaccines mandatory?

☐ Should it be mandatory for doctors trained in the UK to work for the NHS for a minimum of 10 years?

☐ Do you think abortion should be legal?

☐ What are the ethics surrounding giving contraception to a 14 year old girl?

☐ What are the ethics of a doctor going on strike?

# Ethics Template

Put the interview question here:

Non-maleficence

Beneficence

Justice

Autonomy / Consent

Dignity

Any other points

Overall, my opion is

# Value of a Human Life

**What are the ethics surrounding spending money on an individual, especially in the NHS? We will explore this topic using the drug *Kaftrio*, which is used to treat cystic fibrosis (CF) and was made available in the NHS in August 2020. Before we explore the ethics on the next page, here is some background on the topic.**

## What is CF?

CF is a genetic disease caused by a mutation in one of the membrane channels that cause the production of sticky mucus in the lungs, digestive tract and reproductive tract.

## What are the complications of CF?

Sticky mucus is the lungs causes recurrent chest infections needing recurrent hospital visits. Over time, this can cause long term lung damage, sometimes to the point where patients may need a lung transplant. Sticky mucus in the digestive tract can cause the pancreas to stop working and can stop the intestines from absorbing food properly, so patients may struggle to put on weight. The sticky mucus in the reproductive tract can causes infertility.

## What are the old treatments for CF?

There is no way to cure CF, but medications are used to manage symptoms and complications. Antibiotics to treat infection and some people can be permanently on antibiotics to prevent infections. Medication are to replace the job of the pancreas like insulin and digestive enzyme supplements. Treatment is given to thin the mucus in the lungs and physiotherapy to help them cough it up.

## What is Kaftrio and how much does it cost?

A new treatment for CF that is a combination of drugs. It works on mutations found in 95% of people with CF. Some predictions suggest that it could cost over £100,000 per person per year, which is a huge amount of money!

# Value of a Human Life

## What are the benefits to the patient to take it?

Kaftrio has been found to:
- Improve lung function.
- Improve quality of life.
- Increase life expectancy.
- Weight gain.

## What are the problems with not giving the medication?

- Frequent hospital admissions, lots of medications and difficulty breathing can cause poor quality of life for the patients.
- CF can causes lung damage and need a lung transplant which costs the NHS money.

## What are the benefits to the NHS/ general population from the drug?

- Free up hospital beds for other people.
- More people with CF can work and participate in the economy.
- Less antibiotic usage decreases the risk of antibiotic resistance for other people.

## What are the drawback to the NHS/general population from the drug?

- The money could be used to treat other people with cheaper conditions to treat, so could help a greater number of people.
- The money could be used to treat infectious diseases, like HIV and TB, which by treating prevents the diseases from spreading to other people.

# Value of a Human Life

**Practice questions:**

Using the knowledge you have learnt from the previous two pages, answer the mock questions below.

*Hint: Refer  to the section on the pillars of medical ethics to help you answer these questions.*

- **What are the ethics surrounding giving patients expensive medication?**

- **What would be the most ethical decision, giving a drug that could extend 10 people's lives by 10 years or giving a drug that could extend 100 people's lived by 1 year?**

- **What are the ethics surrounding patients paying full price for their medication?**

- **Should there be a limit on how much money is spent per person in the NHS?**

- **What may be the consequences of privatisation of the NHS?**

# NHS AND HEALTH TOPICS

Knowing about the NHS and why it has been in the news is a common theme in interview questions. By going through our list of NHS hot topics on the next page, you can prepare for your interview and demonstrate to your interviewer that you have the knowledge of the NHS, how it works and the problems it faces.

In the following chapter, we discuss:
- Antibiotic resistance
- Type 2 diabetes
- Dementia
- Measles
- Stop smoking campaigns
- Sugar tax
- Organ donation
- 7 -day NHS
- NHS in the winter
- Metabo law
- Postcode lottery
- Virtual and phone consultations
- Aging population
- What is in the news?
- COVID-19 practice questions

# Antibiotic Resistance

Antibiotic resistance is the ability of bacteria to develop evolutionary adaptations to protect them from the antibiotics we use to treat bacterial infections. Antibiotic resistance is a growing problem globally. In the UK, at least 12,000 people die each year due to antibiotic-resistant infections, which is roughly the same as the number of people who die from breast cancer each year.

**What causes antibiotic resistance?**
- Increased use of antibiotics allows bacterial species to mutate and develop mechanisms to protect them from the antibiotics.
- Overuse of antibiotics when they are not needed, e.g. for viral infections in the GP setting.
- Spreading of antibiotic resistant infections in the hospital.
- Overuse of antibiotics in the meat industry allows resistant bacteria to be transmitted to humans.

**What has the government planned to do in order to control antibiotic resistance?**
- Decrease antibiotic prescribing in GP.
- Aim to decrease antibiotic use by 15% by 2024.

Now your turn. Here are some questions to think about:
- **How can we tackle antibiotic resistance?**
- **What are the ethical considerations surrounding not prescribing antibiotics to someone with an infection?**

# Type 2 diabetes

Millions of people in the UK have type 2 diabetes and it increases every year. It is where your body cannot regulate the blood sugar levels properly and is partially due to lifestyle factors such as obesity, sedentary lifestyle, not exercising, eating sugary foods, and high calorie intake.

**Risk factors for developing type 2 diabetes:**
- Family members with diabetes
- Being overweight or obese
- Smoking
- Eating unhealthy foods
- Not being active
- Being a high risk ethnicity

**Complications of type 2 diabetes:**
- Infections
- Kidney disease
- Eye problems and blindness
- Heart disease
- Stroke
- Nerve problems

Now your turn. Here are some questions to think about:
- **What do you know about type 2 diabetes?**
- **What impact does type 2 diabetes have on individuals and the general public?**
- **Should people with lifestyle diseases pay for their own treatment?**

# Dementia

Dementia is an umbrella term for a group of conditions which mostly affects the elderly and causes cognitive impairment resulting in impaired memory and overall function. The most common form of dementia is Alzheimer's disease. Dementia is a progressive neurodegenerative disease which means it worsens over time and cannot be reversed. The incidence of dementia is increasing worldwide as more people are living to an older age. This is particularly true in the UK where almost one-fifth of the population is aged 65 and over.

**Symptoms of dementia:**
- Memory problems
- Change in language and communication
- Problems with concentration and planning
- Changes in personality
- Difficulty with problem solving
- Difficulty with everyday tasks including eating and washing
- Patients may not be orientated to place, time or person

Now your turn. Here are some questions to think about:
- **How would you approach explaining something to someone with dementia?**
- **How do you think dementia affects the person and their family?**
- **Who do you think should make the treatment decisions of a patient with dementia?**

# Measles

Measles is a highly infectious disease where one person can infect up to 14 people on average. It is a serious illness and causes long term morbidity and mortality, affecting multiple systems in the body including the lungs and brain. It most commonly affects children and there is a high risk of serious complications and death in vulnerable people such as children, pregnant women and immunocompromised individuals.

**MMR vaccine:**
Measles is also a highly preventable disease, thanks to the introduction of a vaccine. The Measles, Mumps and Rubella (MMR) vaccine offers protection against measles and two other similarly serious infectious conditions with a high morbidity and mortality rate.

The MMR vaccine is given to children at the age of 1 and 3 in the UK and has been shown to provide lifelong immunity. It can also be offered to adults who did not receive the vaccine as a child. The highly successful vaccine programme has dramatically reduced the incidence of measles in the UK. In fact, in 2017 the UK was officially measles-free, although unfortunately in 2018 it lost this status.

Now your turn. Here are some questions to think about:
- **Why do you think the UK lost its measles-free status in 2018, and what can the government do to combat this?**
- **Should people be legally obliged to take up vaccines?**

# Stop Smoking Campaigns

**How does smoking affect the body?**
- Lung damage and diseases (e.g. lung cancer)
- Cardiovascular diseases (e.g. heart attack and stroke)
- Blood blots
- Lung infections (e.g. pneumonia)
- Pregnancy complications
- Passive smoking (e.g. children)

**What is smoking cessation?**
Smoking cessation is the name given to the support offered to help people quit smoking.

**What has the government done to reduce smoking in the UK?**
- STOPtober
- Free NHS Quit smoking app
- Stop smoking clinics at GP practices
- Free stop smoking hotline
- Affordable/free nicotine replacement therapy (e.g. gum, spray)
- Rebranding of cigarette packages to deter people
- Making cigarettes harder to purchase by hiding behind wall in the shops
- Free e-cigarettes in A+E (trial being done in some parts of the country)

Now your turn. Here are some questions to think about:
- **What are the impacts of smoking to the NHS?**
- **What is the government doing to help people quit smoking?**
- **Should we stop funding treatment for smoking-related diseases in the NHS?**

# Sugar Tax

The sugar tax is a UK tax law aimed at certain products with a high sugar content. If a soft drink has more than 5g of sugar per 100ml, the consumer will be charged tax of 18p-25p per litre. The sugar tax was introduced in 2018 to help reduce the rates of type 2 diabetes and obesity in the UK.

## What are the health impacts of sugar consumption?
- Poor dental health
- Type 2 diabetes
- Heart disease
- High blood pressure
- Obesity and associated risks (e.g. cancer)

## How does the sugar tax work?
The theory is that paying more will make people more likely to choose options with less sugar such as water. If this happens, the individual benefits from a lower risk of health complications. On a bigger scale these benefits can be translated to the population. It is also an incentive for the manufacturers to make low sugar alternatives to encourage people to buy their products. Public Health England found that introduction of the sugar tax reduced the amount of sugar in soft drinks by 29%.

Now your turn. Here are some questions to think about:
- **What are the ethical considerations in introducing the sugar tax?**
- **What alternative methods can be used to cut down the rising rates of diabetes and obesity?**
- **What is the argument against the introduction of the sugar tax?**

# Organ Donation

**Organ transplantation in the UK:**

When someone goes into organ failure, they may be eligible for an organ transplant in order to help prolong their life and/or improve their quality of life. The most commonly transplanted organs in the UK are: kidney, heart, liver and lung.

Transplants are given to patients who satisfy a complicated eligibility criteria which includes matching the organ to prevent rejection. Other criteria include co-existing medical conditions, alcohol and drug use, and how urgently the patient needs the organ. These can be bypassed if the transplant is from a live donor who often known the person receiving the organ. However, it is illegal in the UK to be pay or bribe someone to donate an organ.

**Organ donation in the UK:**

As of the year 2020 organ donation has become an opt-out system in England. This is where everybody over the age of 18 is assumed to be an organ donor unless they specifically choose to opt-out, or a family member of the deceased declines.

This was done following a similar law passed in Wales that found the opt-out system increased the amount of organ donations while still allowing people to consent.

Now your turn. Here are some questions to think about:
- **What are the ethical considerations surrounding the opt-out system for organ donations?**
- **Should people be paid for living organ donations?**

# 7-Day NHS

**Current NHS:**

- 24/7 Accident and Emergency access.
- GP services on weekdays, with selected emergency GP services out of hours and on weekends.
- Hospital clinics run on weekdays.
- Operations happen on weekdays, except for emergencies out of hours and on weekends.

**What is the 7 day NHS?**

- A study in 2012 found patients were more likely to die on weekends than on weekdays. Following this the then Prime Minister David Cameron first proposed the idea of a 7-day NHS and planned for completion in 2020. Not all elements of this plan have been successfully implemented thus far.
- Includes 24/7 urgent care services including the NHS 111 telephone service.
- Includes GP services running all week and later into the evening, including the weekends.
- Includes hospitals being staffed the same on weekends as on weekdays.

Now your turn. Here are some questions to think about:
- **What are the pros and cons of a 7-day NHS?**
- **What are the logistics required to successfully make the NHS run for 7-days a week?**

# NHS In The Winter

**The NHS winter crisis is a popular topic in the news every year.**

**Why do you think this is?**
- Increased admission of particularly elderly patients due to winter viruses (e.g. influenza).
- Increased admission of other vulnerable patients (e.g. homeless or those in poor housing).
- Injuries from snow, ice and wet conditions (e.g. falls and road traffic collisions).
- Healthcare professionals get unwell too, and the rates of staff sick leave rise in the winter.

**What is the consequence?**
- The shortage of staff and high number of patients creates a backlog of work which means patients may not be discharged on time.
- As a result, the number of patients in the hospital build up, which means that there aren't enough beds to admit new patients to.
- Not having enough beds means that new patients have to wait longer to be admitted to the hospital.

Now your turn. Here are some questions to think about:
- **What are some ways to tackle the winter crisis in the NHS?**
- **What are some of the issues of long waiting times?**
- **What are the ethical considerations of leaving patients waiting in ambulances?**

# Metabo Law

**What is the Metabo law?**

The Metabo Law was introduced in Japan in 2008 to combat increasing rates of obesity and type 2 diabetes. The law required people aged 40-75 to undergo annual waist circumference measurements. Employers were asked to use their health insurance to fund weight-loss classes for people found to be overweight or obese, or for those who met other criteria. If targets were not met, financial penalties were given to employers or local governments.

**Why was the Metabo law introduced?**

Japan was experiencing a rise in the rates of obesity and type 2 diabetes with the increased adoption of a heavily processed foods. Japan also has an ageing population which leads to an increase in healthcare expenditure on people as they get old. To make matters worse Japan also has low fertility rates which means there are fewer younger people to work and pay taxes to fund the healthcare system.

Now your turn. Here are some questions to think about:
- **What would be the potential impacts on the individual if this law was introduced in the UK?**
- **What are the ethical considerations of introducing a similar law in the UK?**
- **What would be a different way to reduce obesity and type 2 diabetes in the UK?**

# Postcode Lottery

## What is it?

'Postcode lottery' is a term to describe how the care you receive within the NHS can vary greatly depending on where you live. This includes access to care, waiting times and service funding.

What this means, is that there is inequality within the services the NHS provides in different areas of the country. This can particularly impact people who live in poor areas of the country, which is especially bad as poverty is linked to poorer health. So not only can these people be more likely to get medical problems, but they may also struggle getting seen and treated for them.

## What are the consequences of this?

A good way to understand how this impacts people is type 2 diabetes. This needs to be well controlled through lifestyle and medication, otherwise it can cause complications such as foot infections that require amputation. Therefore, if there are disparities in diabetes treatment, this can lead to a greater rate of foot amputation. This was found in Northamptonshire area, where the rate of foot amputations for people with type 2 diabetes was 2.6 times higher than in Lincolnshire area. This is just one example, however it is important to remember that disparities in NHS services effects many aspects of health across the country.

Now your turn. Here are some questions to think about:
- **What is your understanding of the term 'postcode lottery' and what are the impacts of it?**
- **How would you approach fixing this in the UK?**
- **What are the ethical issues surrounding the 'postcode lottery'?**

# Virtual And Phone Consultations

**What is it?**

Consultations between doctor and patient usually occur face-to-face. However, during the COVID-19 pandemic, there has been a dramatic increase in the amount of consultations done over the phone or via online video call, particularly in GP services.

This allowed patients to have minimal face-to-face interaction with their doctor to minimise the spread of the virus. However, there are discussions about what should happen after the pandemic regarding non face-to-face consultations.

The main issue is examining the patient. This can be done visually over virtual consultation e.g. for a rash but for conditions that require physical examination like a lump these patient may then be brought into the GP. However, because most of the talking has already been done over the phone, this can take less time than a traditional face-to-face consultation.

Now your turn. Here are some questions to think about:
- **What issues are currently being faced by the GP services and how will phone call and virtual consultations impact these?**
- **What group of people do you think will benefit the most from phone call and virtual consultations?**
- **What could be the negative impacts of non face-to-face consultations?**

# Ageing Population

**What is it?**

The population in the UK is gradually becoming older as the life expectancy in the UK increases. When people age their body can become more susceptible to certain diseases, which can put pressure on the NHS.

**What are medical problems seen in the elderly?**

- Dementia
- Arthritis
- Falls (can cause things like fractures and head injuries)
- Infections (e.g. UTIs and pneumonia)
- Heart disease and strokes
- Cancer
- Mental health issues (many elderly people can be house bound and isolated and can become lonely and depressed)

**How are elderly patients different to younger patients?**

- May have dementia, hearing impairment or vision impairment so may need support communicating.
- They may have multiple conditions or be on multiple medications making them more complex to treat.
- They can be less fit so become more sick or take longer to recover than younger patients.
- May need more support when being discharged from hospital such as arranging carers at home or needing to go to a care home.

Now your turn. Here are some questions to think about:
- **How will an ageing population impact the NHS?**
- **How can we improve the health of the elderly population and minimise their impact on the NHS?**

(HINT: Think about vaccinations and the role of a GP)
- **How would you communicate with an elderly patient?**

# What Is In The News?

Sometimes in interviews they can ask you about a medical topic that has been in the news recently, usually in the last month. So this is going to show you how to do this research.

**Where to find it from?**
The BBC is a good place to start and the NHS website has a section for news. These will be tailored towards the general public. You can also look in scientific journals such as The Lancet or the BMJ however these will be more scientific.

**How to tell if its good?**
Not all sources of news are reliable - refrain from using Tabloid newspapers which tend to have more opinions and less facts. Be careful of 'clickbait' headlines, which are often misleading and lack scientific basis.

**What topics to pick?**
You want to try and avoid topics that are too obvious. Remember that every question will be asked to hundreds of candidates so you want to stand out, so try and pick a topic you know well enough while still being something other people may not know about. It's also good to show passion, so if it is an area you find interesting it will be much easier for you to talk about it.

**What to remember from it**
It is a good idea to know about some important statistics as well as a little bit of background of the topic, why the research was done and what does it change in the field.

**What questions can they ask about the topic?**
They may ask a bit more about the topic background. For example, if it's a topic about growing kidneys in a lab from stem cells, then it will be good for you to know what are the roles of the kidneys and what are the current treatment for patients with kidney disease.

# COVID-19 Practice Questions

COVID-19 may be brought up as ethical, factual, reflective or lateral thinking interview questions, or even (more likely) as a combination of these. Remember to answer the question and try not to get side tract, explain your thought process and use key words where possible.

**What do you think will be the long term impacts of the pandemic?**

**How has the pandemic influenced your decision to go into medical school?**

**What are the ethical implications of making COVID vaccination mandatory?**

**How do you think the COVID pandemic has influenced the general public's perception of doctors and the NHS?**

**How has mental health been influenced by the pandemic?**

# REALITIES OF BEING A DOCTOR

Knowing what a life of a doctor is actually like is crucial for applying to medical school. This is because if someone is uninformed about the realities and challenges of medical training and being a doctor, then they are more likely to struggle with coping and drop-out of training. This is why it is a common interview topic as medical schools want candidates who are aware of what training is like, which makes them more equipped to face the challenges.

Therefore reading this chapter and having good quality work experience will help you truly assess if medicine truly is for you and how you can communicate that to the interviewer.

In this chapter, we discuss:
- Medical training in the UK
- Different medical specialties
- Who doctors work with
- Easily confused terms
- Multidisciplinary teams
- Teamwork and leadership
- The difficulties of medicine
- Dealing with mistakes and feedback
- Breaking bad news

# Medical Training In The UK

It is useful to understand the different stages of medical training and how long they are. This is a good way to demonstrate your understanding of medical training if asked in interview.

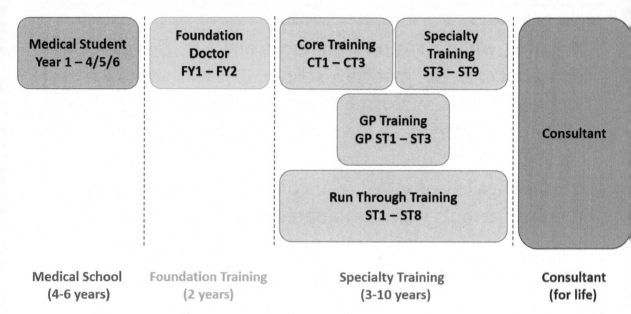

| Medical School (4-6 years) | Foundation Training (2 years) | Specialty Training (3-10 years) | Consultant (for life) |

## What is a junior doctor?

The term 'junior doctor' includes trainee doctors at various points in their training. From the point someone graduates from medical school and starts foundation training, until they complete specialty training and become a consultant, they are known as a junior doctor.

## Can training be longer than shown in the diagram above?

The training duration mentioned in the diagram is the minimum time it takes to become a consultant. Training can be prolonged for various reasons. Some doctors may take the time out for maternity leave, childcare responsibilities or just because they want a break from medicine. Other doctors may want to do postgraduate level qualifications like a Masters or PhD, or to conduct research. There is also the possibility to work less than full time (LTFT) for a multitude of reasons which also prolongs training.

# Different Medical Specialties

*This list is not exhaustive. Refer to the NHS website to learn more about other medical specialties.*

## Surgery

**Job role:** Surgeons operate on patients, and treat different conditions based on their area of expertise.

**Sub-specialties:** General surgery, Obstetrics and gynaecology, Neurosurgery, Cardiothoracic surgery, Trauma and orthopaedics, Otolaryngology (ear, nose and throat), Paediatric surgery and many more

## Internal Medicine

**Job role:** Doctor in hospital medicine, treating a variety of conditions based on the different organ systems in the body.

**Sub-specialties:** Cardiology, Neurology, Gastroenterology, Endocrinology, Nephrology, Dermatology, Geriatrics, Haematology, Oncolgy, Palliaitive Care and many more

## Paediatrics

**Job role:** Doctor in the hospital and community, babies from the point of birth until they turn 18 years of age.

**Sub-specialties:** Similar to internal medicine but with people under 18, Neonatology (newborns), paediatric intensive care

## Psychiatry

**Job role:** Doctors working in the community and hospitals, look after patients with mental health issues

**Sub-specialties:** Community psychiatry, Child psychiatry, Adult psychiatry and many more

# Different Medical Specialties

## Emergency Medicine

**Job role:** Doctor in the hospital who specialises in treating emergency conditions and patients who are acutely unwell when they attend the hospital.

**Sub-specialties:** Pre-hospital medicine, Helicopter emergency medical service (HEMS)

## Radiology

**Job role:** Doctors who specialise in imaging (X-ray, CT, MRI, Ultrasound) and report on images which are taken to make sure patients have the correct diagnosis.

**Sub-specialties:** Interventional radiology (perform minor surgery where they put wires and cameras in the body to take photos and performing biopsies)

## General Practice

**Job role:** Doctors working in primary care, look after day to day wellbeing of their patients when they are outside the hospital, and look after multiple generations of patients.

**Sub-specialties:** GPs see everyone, but can have special interests where they can see conditions of their interest (e.g. diabetes, dermatology)

## Anaesthetics

**Job role:** Doctor in the hospital who specialises in keeping the patients asleep, comfortable, pain-free and stable during the operations.

**Sub-specialties:** Cardiac anaesthesia, obstetric anaesthesia, neuro-anaesthesia and many more

# Who Doctors Work With

*This list is not exhaustive. Refer to the NHS website to learn more about other healthcare professionals working in the NHS.*

## Nurses
**Job role:** Are the main carers of the patients in hospital. They do many jobs including being in charge of monitoring the patients, preparing and giving medication, alerting the doctors if the patient deteriorates and helping patients with daily tasks if they are unable to do so.
They can also be specialised nurses: diabetic nurse, wound care nurse, asthma nurse, epilepsy nurse etc

## Radiographers
**Job role:** Take images of patients using machines. They can also report on findings in the images.

## Midwives
**Job role:** Monitor women throughout their pregnancy and give advise and answer questions. Aid pregnant women in labour. Help women with breast feeding.

## Physiotherapists
**Job role:** Help patients with movement to help rehabilitate them after injury or disease. Can help people with breathing in

## Pharmacists
**Job role:** Help with patient's medication, especially complex medication or patients on multiple medications.

# Easily Confused Terms

## Radiologist vs Radiographer

**Radiologist:**
They are doctors who choose to specialise in imaging (X-ray, CT, MRI, Ultrasound). They generally report on the findings in the images to make sure the patients get the correct diagnosis. Radiologists can also specialise in Interventional Radiology where they do minor surgeries by putting in wires and cameras into the patient and taking images and doing biopsies.

**Radiographer:**
They are not doctors, but one of many different allied healthcare professionals who work closely with doctors. There are two types of radiographers.

Diagnostic radiographers: Specialists in imaging (X-ray, CT, MRI, Ultrasound). Radiographers are responsible for taking the actual image and making sure the correct image is taken from the correct angles to give the best views.

Therapeutic radiographers: Specialists in radiation and radiotherapy. They are responsible for giving radiotherapy to cancer patients and work closely with the patient through their treatment journey.

# Easily Confused Terms

**Physiotherapists vs Occupational Therapists**

**Physiotherapist:**
Work closely with patients and their families to provide physical therapy as a form of rehabilitation. Physiotherapists work in the hospital and in the community. They can subspecialise in to improve strength and conditioning such as musculoskeletal and rehabilitative physiotherapy. They can also work to with patients who have lung diseases such as cystic fibrosis, and neurological diseases such as stroke or multiple sclerosis. Physiotherapists work alongside all the specialties of medicine.

**Occupational therapist:**
Work closely with patients and their families to provide physical supportive measures to ensure the best quality of life and safe functioning of patients. Occupational therapists generally work in the community but are also involved with patient care and discharge planning in the hospital, to ensure all the right supportive measures are placed at home. Examples of the supportive measures they provide include chairlift, ramp and handrails in the shower, but there are many more types of support they provide.

# Multidisciplinary Teams

**What is a multidisciplinary team?**

Multidisciplinary team (MDT) are teams of different healthcare professionals who all work together to achieve provide good patient care.

**What are the strengths of an MDT?**

An MDT is a group of individuals who are all experts in their fields. The benefits of MDT input mean people bring to the table their experience, skills and perspectives. It therefore ensures patients get the best quality of care in an efficient manner.

**What patients are best managed in an MDT?**

MDTs work across many different departments across the hospital and the community. Examples of patients who require MDT care are patients who have **stroke, cancer, hip fracture, elderly patients, surgical patients, mental health patients, patients at the end of life,** and many more. MDT input is required in all specialties across medicine.

**What makes a good MDT?**
- Good communication
- Flat hierarchy
- Safe place to talk about mistakes
- Understanding other peoples strengths ad weaknesses and what they bring to the team
- Everyone feeling comfortable asking for advice and help

# Multidisciplinary Teams

## What is an example of an MDT?

If we use the example of a stroke MDT.

- A **stroke doctor** to diagnose and treat the patients and oversee their care
- A **radiologist** to look at brain scans and help with the diagnosis
- A **physiotherapists** to help patients with strength and rehabilitation
- An **occupational therapists** to help patients function appropriately and safely, and to help put appropriate measures in place for when the patients are discharged
- A **speech and language therapists** to ensure patients can eat and drink safely and are able to speak
- A **pharmacists** to help ensure safe prescribing of medicines
- **Nurses** to carry out the day to day care of the patients on the ward.

Don't forget all the other important members of the healthcare team such as the **porters** who move patients to/from scans and around the hospital, **radiographers** who take images of the patients and help diagnose them such as with a CT scan, the **paramedics** who bring patients into the hospital, particularly in the case of a stroke where they have to act very quickly, **dieticians** who make sure patients are getting the appropriate nutrients to prevent loss of muscle, **GPs** who take over the care once the patients are discharged and look after them in the long term, and many more members of the healthcare team without whom the NHS would not function.

# Teamwork and Leadership

Teamwork and leadership are common themes assessed in interviews as they are important qualities for health care professionals.

When being asked about teamwork, you may not specifically be asked about whether it was in a healthcare setting. If you have experience of working as a team within the healthcare setting, this is invaluable and you should aim to talk about this. If however, this is not specified and you do not have experience in a healthcare setting, you can discuss non-healthcare setting examples, as long as you relate it to a career as a doctor.

Your options include for example being on a sports team, doing group projects, voluntary work like being involved in the National Citizen Service (NCS) or other extra-curricular activities like the Duke of Edinburgh Award. There are many options of what you can talk about here.

The important thing here regardless of your type of experience, is to discuss what you learnt about teamwork or leadership, and how you will improve yourself in the future. A big mistake that candidates often make is to spend too much time describing the scenario, which often adds very little to your mark. It is advised that you should spend most of your time reflect on what you have learnt and how it relates to working as a doctor. See our section on reflection and use the template to practice.

# Teamwork and Leadership

Below are some mock questions to practice through. When discussing something you have done or witnessed, make sure to use the reflecting structure, don't get side tract and bring it back to medicine when you can.

**What do you think is the most important factor in a well-functioning team?**

**Do you think it is more important for a doctor to be a leader or a follower?**

**What makes a good leader?**

**Tell me of a time you had to work in a team and what you learnt from it.**

**Who do you think would be in a stroke MDT and what role would they play?**

**Give an example of a time when you were a follower.**

**Give an example of a time when you were a leader.**

**What did you learn from your work experience about teamwork?**

# The Difficulties Of Medicine

Having unrealistic expectations about medical school and being a doctor is a common reason why people get rejected from medical school. There are many things that doctors have to struggle with and medical school can be very challenging, so if you are not prepared for that, even if you do get an offer, you will be at risk of dropping out.

**Difficulties of medical school:**
- Self directed learning.
- Vast depth and breadth of knowledge.
- Living away from your family and friends.
- Living independently.
- Dealing with exam stress.
- Having to adjust your way of learning.

**Difficulties of being a doctor:**
- Trying to find a good work life balance.
- Seeing death and hardship.
- Long hours and on-calls.
- Long training pathway.
- Having to move location.

**Practice questions:**
*(these should be approached with a reflection structure)*
- **Tell me about a downside of being a doctor that you saw on your work experience.**
- **What aspect of being a doctor do you think will be most challenging for you?**
- **How do you plan on managing the workload of medical school?**

# Dealing With Mistakes And Feedback

Handling failure is a topic that is becoming more prevalent in medical school interviews as well as interviews for doctor specialty training. In medicine, throughout your career you constantly receive feedback from your peers and seniors and often have to do self reflection. Because of this, many medical schools assess how you have responded to failure in the past, or how you would approach potential scenarios in the future in which you are faced with failure, a mistake or constructive feedback. This is a similar structure to reflecting which we have already gone through, but here are some further tips and practice questions.

## Questions to ask yourself
- What were the factors that led to failure that I could not have controlled?
- What were the factors that led to failure that I could have controlled?
- How would I approach this differently if I did this again?
- What skills could I learn to prevent failure if I did this again?
- Who could I get feedback/advice from?

## What not to do
- Do not take feedback or failure personally.
- Do not avoid that task for fear of failing again as you will not improve.
- Do not lie about mistakes you have made, shift responsibility of your actions  or lie bout gaps in your knowledge.

## Practice Questions
- **How do you cope with failure?**
- **Tell me of a time where you worked towards a project that failed.**
- **How do you approach self improvement?**
- **What is the wrong way to handle feedback?**
- **Tell me of a time you felt like you were out of your depth.**

# Breaking Bad News

Breaking bad news is a reality of medicine which is often talked about in interviews. Breaking bad news can be challenging due to the nature of the conversations, and can often be emotional. Some medical school MMIs can involve roleplays and breaking bad news can come up in the form of a roleplay. Other interview questions may get you to talk through how you would break bad news and the good and bad ways to do it. This can be a good way of assessing your understand of breaking bad news, where as role plays assess your communication skills in practice and your ability to stay calm under pressure, especially if the actor becomes angry.

It is also good to know about this as an applicant because this is something doctors do on a daily basis, and knowledge of what breaking bad news is reflects your understanding and passion for wanting to become a doctor.

Many people think that breaking bad news refers only to breaking the news of certain diagnoses like cancer, and death. However, in reality bad news is anything which can upset the patient. On one hand this can include informing a patient that their appointment has been cancelled or telling them that their discharge will be delayed. On the other hand this can involve breaking the news of a cancer diagnosis. All of the scenarios above have the potential to upset the patient or their family, therefore care must be taken on breaking bad news in an appropriate way. Some scenarios may not even be medical, they may involve breaking bad news to a friend when you have made a mistake.

# Breaking Bad News

**How to approach breaking bad news:**

**Setting:** Think about the setting. Choose an appropriate setting where the individual (or people) have privacy. On a hospital ward this might be a small room on the side not in front of other people. Ensure the recipients of the news are seated. In a role play, it is important to sit down. If the person stands up and starts pacing around in frustration, it is important for you to stay seated and remain calm.

**Warning:** Sensitively approach the topic and say you are about to give some bad news at the beginning, to prepare them for what will follow.

**News:** Break the news sensitively. It is important to be honest about the news you are breaking. Apologise particularly if a mistake was made.

**Silence:** Say nothing and use silence as a tool and give the other person time to take in the information and respond. There may be an emotional response. Give them time to appreciate what has been explained to them.

**Empathise:** Offer empathy towards the other person and acknowledge the difficulty of the situation. Saying things like "I'm sorry" goes a long way in offering empathy and comfort.

**Support:** Offer support and allow them to ask any questions if they have them. This may be where you explain how you plan to correct the situation if a mistake has occurred.

**Common mistakes to avoid:**

- Becoming angry or emotional. You want to remain calm.
- Being defensive or making up excuses instead on focusing on an apology.
- Lying or shifting the blame onto someone else.

# Breaking Bad News

**Here is an example of how to break bad news.**

*Scenario: You borrowed your friend's laptop, but accidentally spilt coffee on it, causing it to stop working.*

- **Setting:** Arrange to see your friend, perhaps in their house. Ensure that you will have privacy to deliver the news.
- **Warning:** Sensitively say that you have some bad news.
- **News:** Tell them that the laptop you had borrowed from them is damaged. Tell them that you accidentally spilt coffee over the laptop and the laptop no longer works. Apologise for your mistake and reiterate that it was an accident.
- **Silence:** Give them time to deal with the news and to respond. They may get angry or start get upset and start crying. Give them time to respond.
- **Empathise:** Tell them that you understand this is a difficult situation, and acknowledge its impact on them. Apologise again for the accident.
- **Support:** Suggest what you are going to do in future to prevent something similar from happening again. Also, if appropriate, suggest how you plan to correct the situation. This may mean paying for the repair work or buying a new laptop. If you cannot pay at the moment then be honest and acknowledge that and suggest another alternative, such as maybe paying small amounts over a period of time.

What you suggest to resolve the situation is less important. The important thing is how you deliver the news and uphold your integrity. Doctors have to always act with honesty and integrity and that is what is being tested in this scenario.

# TALKING ABOUT YOURSELF

Talking about yourself is something that some people find difficult. It can be hard to balance selling yourself as a good candidate while being realistic and honest about your flaws and room for improvement. At the same time, you want to avoid sounding over-confident or unintentionally negate the qualities of other people.

It can also be hard because where these questions can be very personal and there is no one correct answer. Instead it is more important to know about structure and how to approach the question, as the questions about you can often be so open that you can take the topic in multiple directions depending on what you want to talk about. Your experiences are unique to you, so although the topics you discuss will most likely also be discussed by other candidates, to stand out you need to give a unique perspective, which is what this section is all about afterall.

In this chapter, we discuss:
- Your personal statement
- Motivation to study medicine
- Extracurricular activities and hobbies
- "Why we should give you an offer?"
- "What if you do not get an offer?"
- What to say if you are a graduate

# Your Personal Statement

Write bullet points to summarise what you mention in each paragraph.

Revise topics you have talked about, especially if you are passionate about them.

e.g. if you have mentioned a book you like, make sure you know it well. If you have mentioned you have an interest in diabetes, make sure you have a good understanding of it.

**Practice doing questions surrounding topics you have talked about.**
e.g. Team work, self improvement, special interests, passion for studying medicine, etc

**General tips for talking about your personal statement:**

- Never lie, as the interviewer may have read your personal statement or have it in front of them.
- Try to practice interview questions around the topic but don't rehearse any answers because the interviewers will be able to tell.
- If you have said that you will do something (e.g. improve a skill, do research or plan to volunteer) make sure that you have actually done it prior to your interview and are confident talking about it.
- Try and get a friend to read your personal statement and ask you questions on it as they will offer a fresh perspective (you will have read your personal statement a few times already)
- Go through these sheets the night before so that everything is fresh on the day of your interview.

# Motivation To Study Medicine

This is a common theme and one that a lot of people struggle to discuss in a way that perfectly captures their motivation while not sounding too generic.

**Common topics discussed:**

- A love of science/the human body: Try and think about what sparked your love of the human body, and why that's important.
- A love of helping people: Try and think about a time where you helped people and what you got out of it.
- A love of human connection: Try and think about a role you played where you had to communicate with people or work with vulnerable people, and what you got out of it.

**Tips on how to approach it:**

- Talk about your experiences. If you have work experience in healthcare which gave you exposure to other healthcare professionals rather than doctors, then discuss this. Talk about what you learn from your experience and why it inspired you to pursue medicine and not another healthcare profession. If on the other hand you have experience of shadowing a doctor, then talk about what you witnessed and what appeals to you with regards to working as a doctor. This will help demonstrate your knowledge of the medical profession and also show your passion.
- If you are going to talk about you or a family member's health then make sure you focus on why you want to be a doctor and not get distracted by the details on the experience of living with a condition or looking after someone with a condition. The important thing here is to relate your experience of receiving care or caring for someone to life as a doctor where you will be providing care.
- Be as honest and specific as you can. Don't be too generic in your answer. For example, mentioning that you want to help people is a good answer, but it is also something hundreds of other candidates will say. To stand out try to add to it and talk about your experience of helping someone, how they benefitted and what you got out of it. Making the answer personal is what makes you stand out as a candidate.

# Extracurricular Activities And Hobbies

Below are some examples of what you gain from hobbies. For each reason, try to think of one of your hobbies that applies to these. One hobby can relate to multiple reasons. When bringing these up in interviews it can be good to talk about an example when when this happened.

- Helps you to develop team working/ leadership skills

- Helps you to develop communication skills

- Allows you to achieve goal and improve at a skill in a non-competitive or timed setting

- Helps you relax after a long day

- Helps keep you healthy while helping you de-stress

- Helps you develop your teaching skills

- Allows you to develop manual dexterity

- Helps you to develop empathy skills

- Helps you build resilience

- Gives you the feeling of accomplishement

# Extracurricular Activities And Hobbies

What is it?

What do you gain from the hobby?

Can you think of an example of a time where it has been useful?

Why is this relevant to medicine?

# Extracurricular Activities And Hobbies

## What is it?

At my school I started a ukulele club where I taught a small group of people how to play songs that they liked.

## What do you gain from the hobby?

I loved being able to socialise with people outside of the classroom, and practicing ukulele both in the club and in my own time was an effective way for me to relax and de-stress.

## Can you think of an example of a time where it has been useful?

During exam season, learning new songs on the ukulele was a good way for me to express myself creatively which prevented me from becoming really overwhelmed with exam stress.

## Why is this relevant to medicine?

Studying medicine and being a doctor can be overwhelming at times and it is important to take a step back and spend some time to relax in order to avoid burnout. Being overly stressed can impact your ability as a medical student and as a doctor. The importance of burnout was highlighted to me at my work experience, where the doctor that I was shadowing explained the importance of a good work-life balance.

# "Why Should We Give You An Offer?"

This question has different ways of approaching it. You can talk about skills you have, experience you have and knowledge you have. You can talk about what gives you enjoyment, how this medical school would suit you and the list goes on. It is relatively easy to do an okay job at the question, but needs skill to answer this in a way that is not only excellent but will also stand out from the other applicants, as most answers can sound very cliché.

Common mistakes when answering this question
- Only talking about one aspect of yourself.
- Talking down other students.
- Giving a vague and cliché answer that will not make you stand out.

On the next page there are some topics that could be covered. For the ones that apply to you, try and expand on them further. Try and make it stand out as much as possible from other candidates by making it personal. Approach this like you would a reflection question.

1. What is the skill?
2. Discuss where you have displayed this skill.
3. Explain how this applies to the medical school you are applying to, being a medical student and/or being a doctor.

# "Why Should We Give You An Offer?"

**Examples of topics you can discuss:**

- Experience in the health care setting.
- Having a previous degree and university experience.
- Good at/enjoy problem solving.
- Good at/enjoy helping people.
- Have a good understanding of the realities of being a doctor.
- You would suit a feature unique to that medical school.
- You have explored other options e.g. work experience in other healthcare fields, taken a gap year, done a degree.
- Good at/enjoy working as a team.
- Dedication to go into medicine.

It is not just what you discuss, but how you make it unique to you.

# "What If You Do Not Get An Offer?"

This question can be asked in medical school interviews because it is a great way of assessing: how do you cope with failure, how well can you reflect on your flaws and improve, your committed to medicine, and if you have realistic goals and back up plans. Also, as medical school placements are hard to get, it is also useful for you think about this ahead of time and to have a plan B.

**Common mistakes include:**
- Being overly confident that you will get a place.
- Overly relying on getting a place at other medical schools.
- Not having a back up plan.
- Just saying 'I will try again next year' without elaborating. This shows that you assume the reason you did not succeed was due to reasons you cannot control, like not enough places, rather than due to a flaw that you need to improve. So talk about how you plan to improve the next time you apply.

The way to approach this question is to think about what are the different reasons why people fail and what the correct way of dealing with them would be.

**For example**
- **Problem:** Lack of work experience
- **Solution:** Spend the following year doing work experience, volunteering or get a job in a healthcare-based career e.g. as a Health Care Assistant

Now try and think about the solutions for the following causes of medical school rejection:
- Insufficient knowledge of teamwork.
- Unrealistic understanding of being a doctor/training to be a doctor.
- Bad communication during the interview/panicking under pressure.

# What To Say
# If You Are A Graduate

Many of you will be applying as a graduate. Some medical schools allow graduates from non-science backgrounds. The interviewers will usually not know whether the candidate is a school leaver, gap year student or graduate entry, and therefore it is important for you to bring this up in your answer where possible.

Here are some of the benefits of being a graduate that may apply to you:
- Exposure to stress, deadlines and time management.
- Exposure to self-directed learning.
- Exposure to learning anatomy.
- Exposure to learning about diseases.
- Exposure to other careers, for example pharmacy or another healthcare profession.

Here are some of the interview questions where you can discuss being a graduate:

- **Why should we give you a place at our medical school?**
- **Why do you want to be a doctor?**
- **What would you do if you did not get an offer?**
- **How to cope with stress/being under pressure?**
- **What skills do you have that would make you a good doctor?**
- **Tell me about a time were you had to improve one of your flaws.**

# THE INTERVIEW

The interview can be a very anxious period, especially for your first interview where you do not know what to expect. Nerves play a big role in how you perform on the day and seeing all the other candidates turn up to the interview can make some people feel very overwhelmed. Read ahead as we discuss the final preparations for the day and share some tips about the interview itself so you are ready for the day.

It can also be your first time seeing the campus or speaking to current medical students at the university. So it is important to use this opportunity wisely and explore the campus and get to know the course, even if you are nervous about the interview. Afterall, if you decide to take the place then you will spending a long time in that medical school so find out about the school and the area as much as you want. This can also help calm the nerves and allows you to socialise and take your mind off the interview.

In this chapter, we discuss:
- The few days before your interview
- Tips for your interview
- Using your time wisely
- Most common mistakes

# The Few Days Before Your Interview

A few days before the interview can be daunting. There may be a lot going through your mind and it is easy to forget some important things. Here is some advice on how to use your time in the last few days.

**Dress code:** Decide on what to wear and prepare for the day. Try to balance professional with comfort as you do not want to be too hot or cold. Often medical schools will indicate on the interview letter or website what dress code to expect.

**Documents:** Know what you need to bring to the interview e.g. invitation letter, identification documents, certificates of qualifications.

**Travel:** Know how long it will take to travel there and plan the journey. This includes finding out where the nearest train station or bus stop is, and the nearest place you can park he car if driving.

**Accommodation:** If you need to book accommodation and haven't already done so, now is a good time to do it. This is particularly important if you need to travel far and require a stay on the night before the interview.

**Medical school and locality:** Read about the medical school and the course as well as the town or city. Think of some interesting points and questions to ask when you go on the tour of the campus and facilities so you get a better understanding of what the student life would be like.

**Light reading:** By now you should have done the majority of your interview preparation, but it may be a good idea to do some light reading, such as reading healthcare-related news, or reviewing your personal statement, or anything else you feel you need to cover. Try to make the reading light and don't over-work yourself.

# Tips For Your Interview

**Have a conversation:** Often in times of stress people can talk too fast or slow, which can be distracting and may take away from the point being made. What sets the good candidates apart is their ability to pace themselves. It is useful to think of interviews as conversations, therefore you should try to pace yourself as if you are having a conversation with a friend. This will engage the examiners while demonstrating your confidence.

**Have a structured approach:** Doctors use structures all the time in practice to make sure that when nerves or time pressure kicks in they have methodically gone through everything that is important. On the day, especially for reflection and curve-ball questions, try and explain your thought process outload in a methodical way.

**Plan your answer:** Before you answer a question, have a quick think about it and plan it in your head. This only requires a few seconds and will help you to structure your answers appropriately and keep time efficient. It also shows the examiner that you are thinking about your response and not rushing to answer the question.

**Reflect in your responses:** It shows that the student has put in the work to learn how to structure reflection, and shows their ability to learn from their experiences, whether good or bad. This is a crucial skill in medicine which involves lifelong learning and improving.

**Link concepts:** Questions will very rarely mention the themes being tested. Candidates who stand out think outside the box and bring in key concepts like medical ethics and the core values. Good candidates will also reflect within their answer. All of this help to make your responses stronger and more thorough.

# Tips For Your Interview

**Refer to sources:** If you have read a book or research article, bring it up in your response even if you are not specifically asked about it. There is a time and a place to mention these things so only bring them up if they relate to the topic in question and make your point stronger. This will help demonstrate your commitment and passion to learning.

**Using time wisely:** What sets candidates apart is being able to use time wisely to return to questions and improve their responses. Once you have answered all the questions on the station, if you have spare time you can return to a previous question and make more points. It is a good idea to return to questions which you think you have not made enough strong points about so you prioritise the quality of responses over the quantity.

**Relax between MMI stations:** Drink water between stations, small sips, as your mouth can get dry and it will help you calm down. Don't think about your last station, it is over and there is nothing you can do so just relax and don't let nerves affect your next station.

**Online interview tips:** Good lighting is important a simple desk lamp will do (but make sure that during interview prep you have got used to it). Make sure you can see your face and upper torso in your laptop camera. Don't use a swivel chair as most people will fidget. Headphones are good for both making you sound clearer and cutting out background noise but make sure you don't breath too heavily into the microphone or let it rub it against your clothing.

# Using Your Interview Time Wisely

- MMIs will often have multiple questions per station so don't waste time on a question if you can tell its not your best work. If you find yourself rambling on about a question, end it and move to the next one. You may be able to come back to the question at the end after you have answered all your questions.

- If you can tell you are rambling or going off topic, pause and summarise your point and try to refer back to the question.

- If you finish all the questions and have time left at the end, go back to previous questions to improve them. Don't just go back to questions you like, but go back to questions you didn't talk about a lot. Sometimes interviewers may say you can go back and answer previous questions, but other times interviewers may not. So if there are no more questions, use the time wisely and go back and improve previous points.

- If an interviewer interrupts you and hurries you while you are answering the question, it usually means that you have already made sufficient points and they don't want you to repeat yourself, but want you to move on so you can maximise the marks you are getting.

- For reflecting questions, don't spend too much time on anecdotes. You will not get marks by explaining the story in detail, but you will be marked on how well you discuss what you learnt and why it is relevant to medicine.

# Most Common Mistakes

- Unrealistic understanding of being a doctor/training to be a doctor.
- Bad communication during the interview or panicking under pressure.
- Lack of knowledge about the medical school.
- Lack of knowledge about the NHS hot topics.
- Not understanding medical ethics.
- Giving generic, vague or short answers without elaborating further.
- Sounding ingenuine or overly rehearsed.
- Forgetting what you put in your personal statement.
- Lying in your personal statement or interview.
- Not using your time wisely and giving short answers.
- Only giving one answer to complex questions.
- Going on side tangents and not truly answering the interview question.
- Not relating the topic to medicine.
- Listing examples without going into detail.
- Not talking about both sides of an argument.

**Try using this sheet like a mark scheme when doing practice stations.**

# REVISION AND PRACTICE

There are multiple practice questions and practice templates scattered throughout the handbook to help you structure your answers. This chapter focuses on helping you revise key concepts and terminology for your interview. At the end there is also an MMI mock.

As well as what is in this chapter, make sure you are up to date with your basic science knowledge that the medical school you are applying for expects from you. Read the information provided on the medical school website as some will tell you what science and mathematics knowledge you need for the interview, if at all.

Once you have familiarised yourself with the structure of answering questions, it is good to practice them in a timed setting so you can practice providing your best answer under pressure.

We have revision pages on:
- Explain these terms
- Recall revision
- Medical training pathway quiz
- Quiz
- Breaking bad news practice
- MMI mock 1
- MMI mock 2

# Explain These Terms

Try and practice defining these terms. To find the answers look at the sections on NHS hot topics, abbreviations and definitions, pillars of medical ethics, and medical research terminology.

(1) **Resilience**

(2) **Dignity**

(3) **Sugar tax**

(4) **Beneficence**

(5) **Gillick and Fraser competence**

(6) **Informed consent**

(7) **Euthanasia and assisted dying**

(8) **Burnout**

(9) **Hollistic care**

(10) **Double blinded**

(11) **Randomised controlled trial**

# Recall Revision

Here are a list of questions. In 3 minutes, answer each question to the best of your abilities. Rate your confidence in answering each question in the real interview out of 10. When the practice is over, research any topics where you have noticed a gap in your knowledge.

What are the impacts of type 2 diabetes? /10

What is the difference between euthanasia and assisted dying? /10

What are the different types of doctors? /10

How is the NHS different during the winter?? /10

What is the role of a GP? /10

What are the impacts of smoking? /10

What is meant by the term '7 day NHS'? /10

What are the advantages and disadvantages of introducing the sugar tax in the UK? /10

# Medical Training Pathway Quiz

Put these in order of training and summarise each role. For the correct answer check our section on 'Medical training in the UK'. Don't forget, it is important to practice verbally saying your answers, even if you are by yourself, as it can help you be more fluent in your answers.

## Consultant

## Foundation doctor

## Medical student

## Specialist trainee

## Core trainee

# Quiz

When is it okay to break confidentiality?

What does an anaesthetist do?

What are the laws surrounding organ transplantation in the UK?

What factors make up a competence assessment?

What factors would make someone unable to give consent?

Who can make a decision about a patient's care?

List some examples of who doctors work with.

What are the pros and cons of phone and virtual consultations?

What are some of the medical problems we may see more with an ageing population?

What are the laws surrounding euthanasia and assisted dying in the UK?

What are some of the way the NHS is helping people quit smoking?

What are some of the problems that come with dementia?

What are the most common causes of death in the UK?

How do vaccines work?

What does the MMR vaccine provide protection against?

What are some of the complications of the flu?

# Breaking Bad News Practice

If you are by yourself or roleplay is not done at the university you are applying to, you can talk through how you would approach the scenario.

**Practice questions:**

- **What makes a good apology?**
- **What makes a bad apology?**
- **Why do you think it is important for a doctor to be able to break bad news?**
- **What may be the consequences of a doctor breaking bad news inappropriately?**

**Role play scenarios:**

- **You need to take another blood sample from a patient after you accidently lost the previous sample. You will need to tell this to the patient.**
- **Your friend spent a month making a painting for their dad's birthday and left it at your house. You accidently spilt water on it and it is ruined. Your friend has now come to pick it up for the birthday tomorrow.**
- **You are working at a fast food shop and the milkshake machine is broken. A customer has come in to collect their order for a children's birthday party. You need to break the news that you cannot supply them with the milkshakes.**

# MMI Mock 1

*For practice purposes, we have set two different time limits for these stations. In the real MMI all stations would be the same duration.*

## Station 1 *(8 mins)*

1. What is your definition of a good doctor?
2. What will you do to achieve your definition of a good doctor?
3. Why shouldn't you become a doctor?
4. Which 3 of the NHS values describe you best?

## Station 2 *(8 mins)*

1. Tell me about the training pathways in the UK for doctors?
2. If you were to start medicine this year, how long would it take for you to become a consultant?
3. Why do you think some people take time out of their training?
4. What could we do to help more women stay in medicine?

## Station 3 *(8 mins)*

1. When may it be acceptable to take away a patient's choice about their treatment?
2. What does the word capacity mean?
3. What are the impacts of breaking confidentiality?
4. HIV treatment cost £14000 per person per year. Should it be given for free in the NHS?

## Station 4 *(6 mins)*

1. Tell me about a book you read that changed your perspective on something?
2. Tell me about a skill you improved.
3. What do you think is the best work experience somebody could get before going into medical school?

## Station 5 *(6 mins)*

1. What impacts does the NHS have on the environment?
2. What do you think will be some of the long-term impacts of overpopulation?
3. What impacts do you think global warming and pollution will have on public health?

## Station 6 *(6 mins)*

1. What are the drawbacks of having poor insight into your mental health?
2. Imagine you are a medical student who noticed a fellow medical student crying when alone. How would you approach this?
3. What would you do if you realised you no longer enjoyed medicine?

# MMI Mock 2

*For practice purposes, we have set two different time limits for these stations. In the real MMI all stations would be the same duration.*

## Station 1 *(8 mins)*

1. Tell me about something you have seen in the news recently and why you found it interesting?
2. What do you think has been the greatest medical advancement?
3. What do you think the NHS will look like in 10 years?
4. What role does social media play in the general public's view of medicine?

## Station 2 *(8 mins)*

1. What makes up good communication?
2. What are the impacts of a doctor being bad at communication?
3. How would you communicate a medical diagnosis to a child?
4. What area of communication would you say you need to improve on the most?

## Station 3 *(8 mins)*

1. Tell me about a part of your personal statement that makes you a good candidate?
2. Why do you want to study medicine here?
3. If you had to change one thing about this university, what would it be?
4. Why do you think people drop out of medicine?

## Station 4 *(6 mins)*

1. What country do you think handled the pandemic best?
2. What do you think will be the long term impacts of COVID-19?
3. How do you think the general public's perception of doctors and the NHS has changed because of the pandemic?

## Station 5 *(6 mins)*

1. What role do GPs play in the NHS?
2. What would you change about how primary care (GP services) are currently run?
3. What are the pros and cons of speaking to a patient over the phone?

## Station 6 *(6 mins)*

1. What do you think are some of the causes behind limited bed space in the NHS?
2. What are the impacts of long waiting times in A&E?
3. A patient was due to have elective knee surgery today. However, this has been cancelled last moment due to a lack of bed space. How would you approach breaking this news to the patient?

**Notes**

# Notes

**Notes**

# Notes

Thank you for purchasing our handbook. We've worked very hard on it and we hope you found it as useful as many of our other clients.

We value your **feedback**, so if you have any feedback or suggestions, please leave us a review.

We wish you the very best for your interviews! We love hearing about your success, so please let us know when you receive your offer.

Printed in Great Britain
by Amazon

26082520R00057